MW01704927

www.pamenarpress.com

Daffod*ls

By Khashayar
"Kess" Mohammadi

for one of the most generous
& talented poets 2 know!

Khashayar Mohammadi

Published by **Pamenar Press**

All rights reserved
© **Khashayar "Kess" Mohammadi 2023**
First Published **2023**

ISBN: **978-1-915341-15-0**
Khashayar "Kess" Mohammadi
Daffod*ls

Cover design and book design:
© **Studio "HEH"**-Hamed Jaberha

www.pamenarpress.com
info@pamenarpress.com

*© Daffod*ls*

All rights reserved. No part of this publication may be reproduced or transmitted in any form or by any means, or stored in any retrieval system of any nature without prior written permission, except for permitted fair dealing under the Copyright, Designs and Patents Act 1988, or in accordance with the terms of a licence issued by the Copyright Licensing Agency in respect of photocopying and/or reprographic reproduction. Application for permission for other use of copyright material including permission to reproduce extracts in other published works shall be made to the publishers. Full acknowledgement of author, publisher and source must be given.

*

when you read this know that I first spoke

when you read this know that I've been speaking.

"Children kneel
In jesus till
They learn the price of nails"
-King Crimson

Daffod*ls
stretched off the tongue
SO MANY WHITES
STILL LEFT IN THE WASHING MACHINE
dream grammar
succ*nct
but pressing!
Deleuze at the mental hosp*tal
edging my dreamscapes
and racing to write
"if you were alive" chats
and an AI generat*on
of someone or something
HYPERNATURAL

Daffod*ls

where blankets can stop the sun
only real in the death sentence
in the life sentence:
minimal plateaux:
slight mountain
            cold sun
through ragged clouds
suckling on this side of language
waking moments indebted to m*nd spent.
and spent on gr*ef,
pomegranate seed
to birdspeech

we're spread too thin
and masked or unmasked
the train ride is just too long
for companionship
so I leave the story on the night that its told
"you had to be there" kinda laughs
"who do u think u r" fingers pointed
and holstered in jackets from frostbite

the book
mentions to risk
and to privilege
is to balm salted wounds with the smell of acac*a
I swear I'm reading up on pedagogy
and by the discussion
I promise I will understand!
and subtitled with an aster*sk
is a muddy delta of sedimented thoughts
with my cat
nibbling on my toes
and hands
Infinite in their capacity for wonder

a bunch of
Daffod*ls
biblically parted
and our dance alone
at the corner of the wine bar
rent is due as it always is
my tongue is paved with
Daffod*ls
they are violently flashing
I could pinch them and
swipe
and swipe
until water

Hey hon! fun fact!
just because you're alone
doesn't mean
you're the sovereign soul of this corpus!
Daffod*ls
are the reason I am the narrator
staring into cat eyes
with my own cat eyes
listen I've tried to explain the
predicament
and failed every time
so I finally acquiesce!
teach me the Greeks!
teach me YOUR Greeks!
I'm friends with asphalt
knees bent speaking to the floor
slowed down in the dust
who would've known
to forget the sweetest memory
I only had to lock it
behind a security question?
USERNAME or PASSWORD wrong

I follow the d*scourse
of which I only understand the shape
and fear
transmitted a certain sadness
across the language barrier
I hold inside me
fearful v*scera
I'm looking for the cure
that persists still
even in the beacon of l*ght
that temple of delusion
of which my language is the root

HEY!
my tongue is rotten
my Xeno-body STINKS!
of damn Daffod*ls!!!
and their gentle explosions behind my eyes
*Curta*n drop*
I'd like to slip this poem into bed
and cover it so my sitcom parents won't notice
help me color in my thoughts
but this time: stay within the l*nes!
I'm plagued by visions
in a dozen different tongues
and "have we done the right thing"
isn't even the right question
a soft... circular... motion: I'm learning
but the p*ano won't stop
even if I plead guilty
stuck in the ON SALE! Void
checkmarked for fast delivery
and amazon packages
bleeding on doorsteps

I'm invited inside a book
and I don't take my shoes off
such is the pearl:
a sed*ment
connecting erogenous zones
Y'know
its all about the masterful evasion of state
and statements
whaddya want me to say?
fraud is damn funny
because it truly clears your throat!

there's no d*stance in dreams
only itch
but not an allegorical one
just skin: scream*ng
tethered to the voice: a game we play
to appear sober for a moment
forgetting the mood swings of w*nter:
death by theorization

its w*nter and the sky is closed for renovation
so I apply for a revolution and am rejected
my undercurrent
is not powerful enough to surface
and when I see myself
as I see myself in the m*rror
when I see myself
as I am on the other side
I think about you sometimes and the doors you built
the l*ght you see through the crevice
and the l*ght you see through
there's a treat*se
in fear of the l*ght may never ever stop

if I told you I haven't been to the mounta*n
where Farhad was sent to dig:
scent of l*ly over rock and rock over snow:
            oh how a landscape can bludgeon!
            how water can brush!
I wash myself ashore an intrusive thought
clinically sharp
as police station lights
that fluoresce this shelter
like the closet door
open for a moment
and awfully inviting

speak to me
simultaneously
speak to me
through the subject/object divide
I attend a celebration
long enough to leave
my smile in the crowd
that moment of listening
and all that comes after
when I take my eyes off the speaker
and wander onto velvet curta*ns
the dynamo spins
and creates sparks
in the failed madness
I was not there when the poem started
will not be there when it ends

Listen!
I arrive early for the poem
after the word but before there is sadness in language
my tongue swells but my words
cannot scale to my teeth
they froth in between
and floss through
flattened

to always be the ground
  /to always be the ground
who is impenetrable?
who is the killing floor of the tongue?
Daffod*ls on the balcony
in the way of the sun

you can pierce a man through his silence
you can look at someone,
 /you can look at someone.

I'm stuck in teeth
I roll in blobs
I see th*ngs
 /when I look at someone

my voice is heavy when gorging on the stars
don't fill up
there are three gas stations left
before Daffod*ls
in me there is a military urge to create
thanks Dad for swaddling me in tree bark!
tonight
I met your darkness and its many curves

every once in a while I respond
to the pol*t*cal question because
the pol*t*cal questions are always easy

Just answer

QUEST*ON!
    I taste change
    in waiting
QUEST*ON!
    on the quietest corner
    of the tongue
                smoking.

when you ask what difference can it make
I'd like to mention
how the tongue is a muscle
and teeth are bones.
like Daffod*ls
imbedded in the skull

I was told a few times
I can't remain neutral
so I grew into an explos*on
of l*ght against l*ght
Daffod*ls
looking up at the slow descent
of the archangel
w*ngs overtaking the sky

the Qur'an
and its insistence on reading lessons
l*ps on a l*pstick
prayers on a pancake
plastic fruit on plastic-wrapped furn*ture

Daffod*ls under a stream of p*ss
the voice that got me and gut me
a baker's dozen sweet Abrahams
climbing up Mor*ah
subl*ngual pills
unable to extinguish accents
in the last moments of waking life

the skipping record
keeps tempo with the light's flicker
and when it got scary in the dark you turned to me
and for a moment we could've slept with each other

some consonants pass through Daffod*ls
others fall to the floor cloud-heavy

the installation smells of Gasol*ne
exhibition texts are too large to read
from any sub-planetary outlook
but y'know
there's something
about the earth's early work
I really like
when it was more conjunctive
the *AND*
and the *OR*
and of course the *BUT*

brace for the itch
brace for all the itches!
when I came here there were still thoughts here
dear Daffod*ls:
WHAT IS THE EASIEST WAY TO AVOID SWEETNESS
                                        there's this practice of restraint
                                         honed only in teeth
                                         the soil that cultivates
                                                  b*tter ol*ves

oh how I wish my voice had no weight
so I could run away between sentences
a small bell jar oozing
with honey
leftover note from
her su*c*de

I'm tired of typing gr*ef into search boxes to define
and you're tired of cross-referencing them with
r*tuals of the old life left behind
        dear Daffod*ls
what's the best way to float when speaking?

        most of my days are spent cleaning the body
         dear soap!
         let's work something out!

why are you silent please speak to me!
the revolution's been spitting us out
                    listening to the morning news I...
                    ...pour hot water into something
                    until it dissolves...

the mysterious back alley gateway to the dive bar
and the bartender's gentle tenure
in the endless n*ght
in the corner of the bus someone has lost something

a dropped hockey puck
in that dull social apparatus
of Trans*t

I am at all times alert of the source text
of which I am an offshoot
caught in the act of poetry
enhanced with vowels that gl*de
surviving by threads of a question:
whether the poem speaks or listens
is your choice entirely!

I'm slowly moving to the other side

I forego the eyes
and speak directly

running on the rim of the pacific garbage patch
sitting
on its unopened sauce packet pen*nsula

and that slow return of students
from recess
the school office
spending its teachers
into the marble-cool corridor

I put up a show
but my self-immolation hardly even makes news
the whole problem is to make it (through)
and make it (last)
don't mistake the page for writing
and don't mistake writing for any semblance of speech
if you look hard enough DAFFODILS can be found
this place can be lived in somehow
appearing at the end of each *nc*s*on
a chest like a book to invest words into

this year I danced many times to crumbling nations
love you Daffod*ls! godspeed your probes!
    in between the second and third thaw
    before last frost but after winter solst*ce
    between each skip of the rope
please lead your reader back inside
the less you speak the more you breathe
                                        in the poem

so much happens in this sk*n.
that's why I keep shaving
if I were to eat myself I'd start at the tongue
they were picking names for FROSH week
I joined team SURVIVAL
nice and sticky in lust and some paperwork

a little spare:
/a little sparse

when I hear something loud I immediately think> Daffod*ls
under pieces of the punctured time card
or the last stamp before free coffee
sometimes I can't guess the time it takes to wish upon a star

when you say things the phone rings
            and I turn around
realizing its important to stay sometimes

when the house falls apart
look at the mothers picking dill inside
and that exhaustion from cooking
                        unlike any other
            what use is an etsy shop
            for a woman that never rests
what use is property to the chronically left behind

you see...
when you start to question Daffod*ls
you start with a mission
and by surprise you get to the truth sometimes
you see... when you get to the truth
no matter how much you work on yourself
the truth still does not like you back sometimes

“It was February
I was cold and I was high” -IDLES

some days I hear s*rens a touch above consciousness
am   I   dead in the next layer
resisting sleep
hand in hand with grandma
sweat dripping down her moustache
carrot/celery/dill
NO BREAD SOLD IN INSTALLMENTS
handwritten ads for black market k*dneys at the kiosk

Daffod*ls are funny
how they spread and
fuck wild
every single time
thoughts organized by landscape
SPEECH ARCHITECTURE
holding down the thrush of slow, but turbulent oceans

its simple: I don't carry with me a sense of men
let's start over and this time let's look at the stars
and their silent revolution
I found it somewhere in those sp*rals
    between pulsar/
        and neuron th*stle brush
      p*ne needles for kindling
      breaking the speed of f*re

d*rect. sunl*ght.
horses bur*ed in sand
GOOD MORNING RESSURECTION
an "Assalamualaikum"
where the dead fall from my eyes

the simplicity of etern*ty
measured only in bl*nks of an eye
we can wait another 20th century
to begin studying Iran
teach me you francophones in the university of Tehran!
a pocket
turned inside out
for any willing robber walking around

meat is too expensive so we load up on the sauce
ketchup-mustard burnt chicken
asphalt crackl*ng like star an*se in ol*ve o*l
I'm single malt double vaxxed triple parked
but still can't afford another hor*zon l*ne
buses lined up at the stop
and the sheer amount of morning it takes
to slurp coffee and move this body to work
y'know...
the dream never came back to ask
for what it had left behind

the moaning column
the weeping podium
mourning the loss of
that sweet Abraham!
(of his
is greatness)
and how Hafez says a heart is affl*cted
with itself
self-blossoming
flower at the p-eo-ple of my eyes
and the anc*ent language of milk
that sweetness of the pre-coca cola times
a god-ray of wine
drinking to the subl*ngus
convivial with Daffod*ls
with l*ps sweet as soda pop
with arms, warm as a centralized furnace
with eyes br*ll*ant as FIFA approved stad*um l*ght

gr*ef creates hobbies and lost friendships start races
school shooters and their side business of al*enation
frozen steaks slapped on the skillet still damp
pint of Guinness pie crumbs
I wanna make my own potatoes out of vodka
dead daddy dream.
hybrid fruit and cum socks.
new daddy dream.
cultures and their ecologies amirite?

antlered pallbearer
edging the peel of the v*nyl
with a stranger downstairs
waiting to take off his socks
rascall mallrat
bending down
till I see dayl*ght

I agree with the s*gn that says
BE RIGHT BACK IN FIVE!
a man builds a wall
and I wish him warmth in the anal canal
a summer night st*cky
on the mattress on the ground

FUNNY how the 12 hour shift can pull you

back into the slums of your m*nd

brown boys catching pigeons for fun

or the streetcar driver

behind that layered glass

and the hulk of the way-too-old held child

asleep in a father's arms

when I said this city needs to die

I was just hungry

walking down Jordan Peterson's street

wondering how long the camera has been qu*et

but y'know what I've always expected surve*llance

in my essay about the downfall of celebrity

and the multid*mensional Kardashian form I'll be

exploring a performative self-involvement you can't recognize

I wish my foot soles were heavier for a solid sleep on the bus

the man circling escorts with a l*pstick

tearing apart hardcovers

for the beautiful women inside

"Democracy killed Socrates"

meaning the Demos- now has too much -Kratos

we live in a city of rats we are their guests leave them treats

we are on their clock an hour early dinner rush

vegan guest cucumber allergy split check apps on mine

all day wristbands to the water park of my body

where a pointed camera makes me look at Daffod*ls

the bar is too dark to read in so we wr*te

work keeps making laundry laundry keeps making the bed

I have no space for humility

lets manifest destiny ourselves out of poverty

let's lift ourselves out from poetry and

sit in penthouses

lets steal w*ne in the name of c*vil d*sobedience

and sit on the bed-bug smeared mattress

reading WALDEN arm in arm

until friends leave

until everyone

and everything

moves out

torto*se shell ashtray tortoise shell eyes

I try to reach him after the birth of his second child

he runs past me and into the night where I wish I could tell him

“you are the reason I wanted to leave this world behind”

I attest: half my words have disappeared from the dictionary

so I guess this is my language now

whats up?

whats wrong?

whaddya need now?

I don't have space right now

its best to write with an erection

stretching the thighs apart for max pleasure

massage the words into the mouth

hum to forget the gag reflex

I regret talking today

I regret having a face

stroked gently

dragging me under

and locked hands

behind shoulder blades

fucked

in embrace of the death dr*ve

its funny when you lose in bed

and look up to say

"I'm different now"

cherr*es popped with cherr*es

fingers circling the question

of where the flame may l*ck deep

.

I've attained something

in our salty tenderness

t*ptoes bubbling

like strawberries

in a champagne glass

gypsum mustard rye

funny how the Nordic giants weren't big

I've been taught the practical uses for concrete

and all the glances accumulated at the bas relief

a sort of...

gusting smell

where dad walks in with a pizza

bumps on the nipple/

suck until you see daylight

how boring to know it all

erectile dysfunction

or all the imagery leading to the pornograph

naked in mid-day

AS IF

where buttons bleed

areolas bruise

AS IF

we're in the business of selling footsteps

my new catchphrase is

"hon! that's a warcrime!"

we have that in common huh? funny.

now pins and needles

thread by thread my sleep

tapping in its own tempo

regardless of how much I move forward

Daffod*ls follow behind

windows opened/

doors now closed

mostly

to vent cigarette smoke

and for hugging the sweet corners of the n*ght

we say goodbye motionless

and the more I move on the page

the faster the face dissolves

into the crowd

Daffod*ls organized a protest

where I earned my face for the first time

I keep circling the anus for answers

to the guilt of surv*val

it never leaves the centre of my Be*ng

not the guilt but the anus

what a myth:
to find a length
that fits

palpable but malleable enough like

how muscles are measured in flex

the angle of divined marble

at the corner of the mouth: sucking

wait what happened there in the br*ne?

hello piercing!

hello halitosis!

an obstacle for air

y'know when people are so beautiful

it just kinda ruins your day?

I couldn't swim/

he just...

left me behind

no matter how many people in the word, the audience only functions in silence: no matter how well how great how long: theater disappears at the moment of the bored spectator's cough: lake, stage, sky and the sun-tenderized skin submerged into "mercury levels dangerously high"

Daffod*ls held against & foretold in the <insert language> 101: Its easy to explain Derrida now lets see if you can prove to me the plosion at the linguistic viscera: intergalactic bling in our sand motes, trans-universal dust in psycho-delia.

Daffod*ls sat calmly by the N*le, lured into the shining of the sun of whom we've only seen its hinter side. I wish the moon would turn around. I wish the ground could taste the salt.

ok ok less talk. ok ok I'm the immovable object to your unstoppable force. aite we get it
SEE WHAT YOU DID THERE? BOUN.DA.RIES!!!!

I love theatre simply because of how it insists on rema*n*ng. on staying. on DWELLING or looking behind. *was it love? no. Kierkegaard.* wow how little do "musings" matter. run-on sentence and retroflex tongue in a heaven-less world: how to burn and how to rot? how to grow gills or how to (in my humble avoidance of water, in this short lull (all of which counted towards the auto-theoretic chant of a future Nirvana (of which on a beach (on its own (in its desert dune sweeping flagella (on its hind-legs and hair high-lit by the sun/

/

/

/I stop...

at the precipice of a new though and scout Daffod*ls.
convey past (Re-) located past (Trans-) lated and Re- Re- Re-chorded De- fine!
and fine-

play and its inadequate reach
or speech standing up for a poem and hearing an echo of only
laughter among foot-lit Daffod*ls. the dead are packaged only
for the living and living languages circulate the exhaust of the
individual right back into the d*vidual.

I gloss over names and step right into conversation: never
understood the numbers that split the subject/object d*vide.
laughter and whoop-ass: the only tin-cans.

my subconscious is trained in the trickle-down. when the
night-field ripens in vision I run the tanto against the night sky:
and wow!
watch it bleed a shepherd's del*ght!

"Does the mirror know to go on forever?"
-Lianne La Havas

execut*ons on borrowed time
early morning moon late day starl*ght
I like my hihats peppery and my snares p*ss drenched
behind the closed door someone's cracking open
pistachios
and further slotting my words into the night
when you read me remember that I only speak at night
when you read me remember that I only speak at night.

some people
leave:
and suddenly I'm convinced
there are no real people around
how strange to touch Daffod*ls
only from memory
but what can I say? I like moonl*ght
we'll know soon enough which of us
speak to me Hafez pls tranquilize
arrest this capitalist lex*con
y'know what Hafez?
this city just simply wastes my time

I'm tired of placing the word gr*ef
in the very center of every page
and then building a poem around
believe it or not I have nightmares of... well...
sitting
lemme tear out the sky!
dog ear it for later
with sweat corroding my underwear
as I stare up at the bank tower
stark against the night sky

some nights

the subway

just... goes on forever

but idk

not everyone likes their life

children

of children

of empty spaces

not yet filled with advertisement

glaciers run away

faster than any Daffod*ls can grow

held hostage in the double-shift fugue

its ok.
lets ask
more than we answer
I don't like strict rules for writing
I don't like form and style and format
I don't adhere to the Daffod*ls style guide
I don't like how the vocative works in English
after all what are Daffod*ls but prescriptions
the data shows with staggering precision
that speech crumbles
when non-referential

Daffod*ls don't grow here anymore
don't run it'll all be sadness sooner or later
          don't worry
        fall down slowly in the line

that dark resignation to loss. how long to run after joy and just find construction cones scattered around. I take out the trash and who knows maybe I'm resilient to pesticide.

some relief comes in the form of needles. I'm defeated by numbers. It simply won't happen. it just can't be that easy, to descend and to fall. concede and retreat.

I miss being firmly sat in the middle of a patch of dirt you can claw into. Its finished. skyscrapers no longer scrape the sky. clouds have all moved out of our town. I used to write differently so speak to me NOW, through the noise my hand is piercing. you've got the right idea, sitting with coffee table magazines and tuned into classical music. the weight of sleep, the emergent shapes in the city's blight. please don't read this as somnolent resignation. I have crumbled my hopes and fed them to the ducks. I spend my day swimming through the city's various excreta. the question forms a poem which can make a poem in the readers response. I learn yielding from plant material, curl like the corner of the bamboo leaf under stress of exhibition. the problem with the question is that once posed, its hard to flip the "you" and the "I".

when you read me remember that I only speak at night

when you read me remember that I only speak at night

Such a Lovely day to have to always feel this way - PORTISHEAD

I touched the subway mystery liquid, praying.

I don't know what trompe l'oeil means I won't look it up

"door must remain locked at all times"

as if the door regrets diverging from the wall

y'know

statistically speaking

we're closer to Daffod*ls

than ever before so...

never underestimate how far a joke will carry us

cut off gestures

entomology of men

(you read that right)

name the breath

right before it cuts off

underground

with sulfurous winds

falling to my knees

at the screech of the streetcar

I have no access to h*story

and its oscillations

I wanna write a teenager's Autobiography

sorry if I've fallen short of theory

lemme reach for the pendulum

lemme reach for the smell

to convince of sweat

to justify dirt under fingernails

with wishes felled and an absence tall

and the slow accumulation of cream

greyed in belly button fluff

the absence of music

frames of my speech

rain on the bus window

at the federal bureau

of self-fulf*lling prophecies

the sultry *hashures* of rain

against the night sky

emotions conquered

only with eyes

and putting the mouth

where my speech

is sucked into metal

I carry with me the language of Grandpa

even when his face disappears behind my eyelids

serving the words

serving something at least

recovery FROM

and that *FROM* aimed towards WHAT

and that *WHAT* dragging...

busy footsteps

to wake up and down the stairs

hell's workout

it always makes a difference

when the voice clears

halfway through the poem

I've been faced with many versions

of my own lex*con

and from it I personally like this version the most

when I speak I clear my throat and in it

I step towards a late night snack

inside/   within/   slee.py.

when you read this know that I've been asleep

you may hear this

you may hear this

you may read this

you may read this

funny

the disappointment of cum

a hand put aside in a trickling claw

petrified and left to dry out

I've always loved the smell

after a long walk:

I gorge on you like a jawbreaker

f*sh single strands of pub*c ha*r

from the dry wall of my mouth

I'm an imposter

just because I never leave the house

I'm an imposter

just because we haven't spoken in a while

I miss the beach

because how long you can spend walking away

looking at jagged rocks that form the outer shell

I miss the beach because once I forgot

how not every hor*zon b*rths the sun

Déjà vu microdose

Am I sufficient?

screams the highway looking at me through the window

Am I sufficient?

said the red haze

and erased me

my neighbor sees me

my neighbors see me

until I come into myself

and hug the railing

its easy to speak when there's no one listening

when you read know that I wrote this at 6:29 PM

when you read this know that each poem is a r*ft

that the begging hand reaches through

stay

stay

I’ll bring you wherever there is speech

no more shortcuts

no more shortcomings

what can I say?

doubt me if you dare!

watching the xmas market fluoresce

hiding in my coffee cup

sweet little cherry pie

sweet mulberry squished

where stray cats sleep

mid X-ember rain

awash in riverside

we never shaved much

wow

these fractals of -longing

pro-longing and that awful feeling

unable to tell

if heartbreak or spoiled m*lk

when, for a moment the bed was a surface

and not a comfort when sank into from memory

Toronto's food does me no good

stand up for me

there are dead Daffod*ls at my feet

its all in the inflection

how well you assert the tears

I don't know what to read to you

dear Daffod*ls

rotting at my feet

where have I seen my words before?

its easy to talk

and easier to be silent

its easy to be a voice

and every frequency of its echo

in general

its so damn easy to live

ballpoint arguments

conforming to the Chicago style guide

I didn’t even hear the gunshot

when I got there Oed*pus was already dead

I broke up

bedevilled by Jazz

lights flickering

on the pavement

so

loud

After Andrei Tarkovsky

I don't remember much

a dog

a puddle

leaking arguments

awash in ancestors

who couldn't give any less of a fuck

to understand a country, just smoke by its r*vers

smoke by r*vers in general

and ask yourself:

what does the murmur of water achieve?

what does the puddle whisper to the dog?

calm.

in plaster.

the building layering on its decades

from stone to fresco to egg-wash

cities overgrown by Daffod*ls

I'm waiting in the middle of the frame for the rain to stop

I enjoy waiting for colors to pay off emotionally

wait a minute

how long can a dog sit still?

not much happens and yes,

cigarette after cigarette I contradict myself

but what does the doll's vacant eyes invent

that I don't in my late winter walk

how do you empty a pool?

how do you fully centre a shot?

its all about unrelenting l*ght

at the arresting moment of wind

heart-ache afterparty

that no one shows up to

no one died

to measure the holidays by

the farther I go

the deeper I nest in simplicity

like how Hafez says

the self is agitated by itself

and I use it to tranquilize

I'm out of rollies

Zoe should have paper

I don't know when

but we slip into the underground

walk through the food court

beautiful view of the royal bank

YOU ARE HERE: red star

there must be animals here that survive

there must be other things

that want to leave this underground life behind

hand holding is an exercise in gravity

there is no weight to matter

just spin

to matter/ to mind

to father/ to find

little Dalek

little AI-bloated automaton

little Boston Dynamic shroud

little late Thursday afternoon

little too brave little too tall

grabbing smiles

leaving my little heart behind

I'm able to triangulate the distance

between canonical gods

when you don't read the words

days pass and daylight wipes

some things dissipate

while others purify

what future?

what new year?

let me assure you

that good CAN come of d*stance

After Bijan Najdi

so tired
such that water wears us
deserted
sunny

I inherited a single plot
so I dedicated my sorrow
to my widow

waiting in the humid ch*ll
and WOW we've aged in the wind

beside that smile:
water boiling
lace napkin rings
dancing

I'm out
watching corpses
and the poverty defying gravity
uprooted Daffod*ls
already in love with the dead
in love with all oozing material

everything gathers dust
off cuts of meat
offal
basket of bread

birthdays and orange peels
dried on the furnace

dug myself a house
thirsty for landscapes
and Styrofoam sky

killed the furnace
faces wr*nkling
counting communal cattle

gendarmes
scriveners
rabbit ears
for the butcher
Namaz
before execut*on
how many steps ahead of the law
the guard
not yet acclimated to cold weather
interrogated by the animals we shot

Printed in the USA
CPSIA information can be obtained
at www.ICGtesting.com
JSHW080936221223
54136JS00002B/7

9 781915 341150